Reflections of the
BIG FOUR

R. J. BLENKINSOP

© 1978 Oxford Publishing Co.

Plates by Oxford Litho Plates Ltd.

Printed by Blackwells in the City of Oxford.

SBN 902888 79 X

Published by Oxford Publishing Co.

8 The Roundway, Headington, Oxford.

PREFACE

The photographs in this book cover the next three years from the end of *Echoes of the Big Four*. It was a period when all Railway Enthusiasts were conscious of the increasing rate that the steam engines we all loved were being withdrawn for scrapping.

There were, however, a lot of interesting scenes to be recorded and although outside the scope of this book I spent many hours on the Narrow Gauge with the slate quarry lines in North Wales.

I have mentioned before the difficulty of seeing trains from all the four regions and that is not including Scotland. It has meant that certain parts of the country have received more than their fair share of attention. Once again the Eastern Region has suffered but I hope you are broad minded enough to enjoy any steam locomotive even if it did not operate near your home.

At the beginning of the book are some more pictures taken south of Crewe and of course are a fraction of what was recorded by the camera on that particular day. It was my habit to photograph every train I could and that included the humble goods train. The result would be an almost complete record of the day's movement as seen within a confined stretch of line and looking back at the pictures today my mind remembers the hard work that was involved.

An early rise and drive for a few hours to be by the lineside before 09.00 and taking anything up to 150 shots before the light was too bad in the evening or the rain came down and put a stop to everything. Between the rushing around and driving to another location before the next train went by, one had to eat and drink, change films and try to keep some form of notebook in operation to record what had been seen and the camera settings. To those of you who have done it you will understand and remember falling into the bath on returning home, totally exhausted.

All the regions had most of their large express locomotives running at this time and in addition there were still quite a few antiques in the smaller classes. **City of Truro** and the Midland Compound were hard at work running excursions for the enthusiasts in much easier conditions than today — no tenders being filled by the local fire brigade or humping sacks of coal.

In addition to the practical side of things the men who drove these two vintage locomotives were probably on steam engines during their working week so were experienced and knew how to keep up a good head of steam. Perhaps more important they were physically fit and able to shoot the coal in to the right place at the right time.

British Railways have often remembered the past glories of the Pre-Grouping Railways and the pictures of the station pilot at Liverpool Street Station painted in Great Eastern livery should bring back a few memories. Whilst my visits to London were made fairly often it was not often that I had the opportunity to get to the mainline stations. The pictures at Victoria were lucky as I was only there for an hour and it must have been at one of the busiest times of the day. Included was the picture of No. 35028 **Clan Line** on the *Golden Arrow* still with us today in preservation but in rebuilt form. It is an engine which I have been very unfortunate in photographing during the last two years as either the sun goes in at the wrong moment or smoke drifts down over the side of the boiler.

Another memory for me at least was the day down on the Somerset and Dorset when No. 53807 was running a special train. Although the photography went with no trouble the physical disaster which occurred is still with me today.

Walking over the rails in Bath shed my foot slipped over the side of a rail and within five minutes my poor old ankle had swollen so badly that it was no longer possible to keep on my shoe. It took three weeks to settle down and fortunately was the left foot which worked the clutch pedal otherwise I do not think I should have got back home. S & D 2-8-0's provide me with a memory that still gives trouble from time to time!

In this volume are a number of pictures of the Isle of Wight railways in steam days and they have a fascination which gladly we can still have around today. One O2 0-4-4 Tank Engine **Calbourne** runs in the summer months from Havenstreet to Wootton just long enough to provide the atmosphere and memories of the Island Railways. I have a feeling that the preservation movement would be advised to keep the mileage short on some of the lines now in use and the Wight Locomotive Society seems to me to have the ideal arrangement for supplying the holiday maker with a worthwhile journey at a sensible price.

Although I have not spent a day by the Southern line near Brockenhurst in the last few years the sheer volume of traffic in steam days always surprised me. One train after another crammed with holiday makers would pass by in both directions.

If you have bought this book you are probably a steam railway enthusiast, a railway modeller or it could be an Industrial Archaeologist. Whatever your interest look at the pictures carefully, as you should with any old pictures, it is surprising what information can be found. Go to some of the locations today and see the difference — Betley Road Signal Box south of Crewe would be a good example — if you could find it!

And so start another browsing session — I hope you enjoy the pictures as much as I enjoyed taking them all those years ago.

1 Whitmore station is visible in the background as No. 46256 **Sir William A. Stanier, F.R.S.** nears the summit of the climb out of Crewe and heads for Stafford.

14 June 1958

2 Looking as if it has recently been through Crewe works No. 46115 **Scots Guardsman** approaches Betley Road signal box and on towards London. The engine is now preserved at Dinting.

14 June 1958

3 In the background can be seen the bridge carrying the Newcastle under Lyme to Market Drayton railway, with the platforms of Madeley station in the foreground. Class 5 No. 44770 is on the down fast heading for Crewe.

14 June 1958

4 The fireman looks out ahead for the next set of signals and No. 46163 **Civil Service Rifleman** is working hard with a 13-coach load on the climb to Whitmore. The cows on the bridge are unperturbed as they go home for milking.

14 June 1958

5 Betley Road signal box with two down trains and on the up slow line a Class 5 heads south — rather a lucky shot. Note the different liveries of the coaches and the full sidings. On the left is No. 46205 **Princess Victoria** and Class 5 No. 45020 on the right.

14 June 1958

6 With a very clear exhaust No. 6020 **King Henry IV** climbs under the road bridge near the top of Hatton Bank. The train is the 17.10 from Paddington to Wolverhampton, the engine having worked up to London leaving the Black Country at 11.35.

8 July 1958

7 Photograph No. 88 in *Shadows of The Big Four* is a view from this same road bridge but the other side of the line. No. 45734 **Meteor** accelerates out of Coventry with the fast for Euston leaving the motor city of the Midlands around 08.00 in the morning.

23 July 1958

8   Quite a crowd of locomotive spotters watch the summer working as the trains pass under the city walls of Chester. Class 5 No. 75013 of British Railways design approaches the city and another train leaves on its way along the north Wales coast.

9 August 1958

9   Stanier 2-6-0 No. 42965 leaves Chester with a holiday extra for Bangor. Note the motor cyclist with a crash helmet which was quite unusual in those days.

9 August 1958

10

This is one of my favourites as it shows a relief to the *Irish Mail* passing the city walls on the slow line. The attraction is the lighting with the exposure calculated for the shadows of No. 45736 **Phoenix,** one of the two 'Jubilee' class engines rebuilt with double chimney and large boiler.

9 August 1958

11

And here we get nearer home, just over the fields from where I live. On a stormy morning a lucky shaft of sunshine catches No. 5019 **Treago Castle** as it climbs out of Leamington Spa with the 10.00 from Birmingham Snow Hill.

9 September 1958

12   I am sorry about the telegraph wires but that should not detract from the splendid sight of No. 5091 **Cleeve Abbey** with the down *South Wales Pullman.* It is shown here approaching Goring station on a very misty morning.

12 September 1958

13   The LNWR 0-8-0 on the left, works the exchange sidings for Keresley Colliery and on the mainline No. 49441 approaches Foleshill station with a coal train from Nuneaton heading for Coventry.

7 April 1959

14 The next day I was up early to see one or two trains near St Neots on the Eastern Region. The first was the 08.20 Kings Cross to Doncaster travelling very fast as it approached St Neots station behind No. 60010 **Dominion of Canada**.

8 April 1959

15 In the evening I was near Hatfield watching the succession of trains leaving London for the north. B1 No. 61082 makes for Cambridge on the mainline and a local stopping train approaches on the relief line. The coaches are in maroon livery and the locomotives black.

8 April 1959

16 Perhaps the cleanest engine was this V2 No. 60862 with a fitted freight and just in time before the sun disappeared behind the clouds on the horizon.

8 April 1959

17 Another day out on the Eastern Region included a visit to Stoke Bank to the south of Grantham. Here is No. 60034 **Lord Faringdon** climbing the gradient with the down *Flying Scotsman*.

23 May 1959

18   When you see the filth coming out of the chimney of a steam engine it
is not surprising that they required a lot of regular cleaning. Many of
the sheds did not have the staff and this V2 No. 60893 looks to be in a
sorry state as it climbs Stoke.

23 May 1959

19   At the top of the gradient is Stoke tunnel and A1 Pacific No. 60125
Scottish Union emerges into the daylight with a northbound express.

23 May 1959

20   This is the scene on the climb up to Stoke from Grantham where a V2 has just failed on an up goods train. As the relief engine No. 60050 **Persimmon** backs gently down to couple up, a fast goes by for London behind No. 60055 **Woolwinder**.

21 Signals are off in both directions as No. 60085 **Manna** comes past the iron ore exchange sidings outside Stoke tunnel and on its way to Peterborough.

23 May 1959

22

This is just outside Grantham near Great Ponton and two 'Pacifics' are seen passing each other in the late afternoon sun. In the foreground is No. 60150 **Willbrook** and an unidentified A3 'Pacific' with three coaches on its way south.

23 May 1959

23

No. 60017 **Silver Fox** has a down freight train as it passes a break in the trees allowing the sun to shine on the top part of the locomotive. Note the Silver Fox on the boiler cladding behind the nameplate.

23 May 1959

24 And now we come to the purpose of the journey, to see the *Stephenson Locomotive Society Jubilee Special* make the ascent to Stoke. Here it is at 75 mph climbing the 1 in 200 gradient behind No. 60007 **Sir Nigel Gresley** which was to reach 112 mph near Little Bytham.

22 May 1959

25 It is quite appropriate to have a 'Coronation' class Pacific on the opposite page to an LNER A4. At this time *The Caledonian* was being worked by No. 46245 **City of London** and here it is approaching Brinklow Station shortly after passing through Rugby at reduced speed.

3 June 1959

26   The next four pictures were taken within a short space of time at Victoria Station in London. 'West Country' class No. 34103 **Calstock** is shown just before departure.

29 July 1959

27 In this picture another train has just left and the banker can be seen hard at work. Note the fashion in the ladies clothes and the brackets for taking the *Golden Arrow* boards on the side of the engine.

29 July 1959

28 Calstock has now left the station and is being assisted up the gradient by 'Schools' class No. 30921 Shrewsbury. 29 July 1959

29 Awaiting the departure of The Golden Arrow is No. 35028 Clan Line looking very smart in unrebuilt condition and of course polished to perfection. It is nice to know that it is in preservation at Hereford and comes out from time to time in the summer months. 29 July 1959

Before taking my train back to Leamington Spa I took a few pictures at Paddington and this one shows No. 5094 **Tretower Castle** leaving with the titled train for Cheltenham and Gloucester.

29 July 1959

this flyover at Weaver Junction. In the afternoon a northbound express hauled by No. 46157 **The Royal Artilleryman** has just passed under the up mainline from Liverpool.

29 August 1959

32

When the Midland Compound was preserved it ran a number of Specials for Locomotive Societies and this one ran from Birmingham New Street to Doncaster to see round the Locomotive works. Organised by the Stephenson Locomotive Society it was stopped by signals just where I was waiting to take a picture at Mexborough. Held for some ten minutes by signals there was time to allow the driver to check round the engine and see that all was in order.

30 August 1959

33

A self-weighing tender is just visible on the left and outside after receiving its final coat of paint is No. 60090 **Grand Parade**. My first and only visit to the Doncaster Works.

30 August 1959

34 Black engines and black sheds do not make easy pictures but 2-8-0 No. 63948 is just ex-works and the chances of seeing it again so clean are very remote. Taken at Doncaster Sheds.

30 August 1959

35 In the afternoon the train continued to York for a visit to the Railway Museum not the one we know today. I suppose this could happen today with the same locomotive by visiting the National Railway Museum and by a different route.

36 ...must have been on Monday early in September as this one is taken at Machynlleth just two days later. No. 7801 **Anthony Manor** has just arrived in the station with the freight from Aberystwyth and will shortly be leaving for Shrewsbury with a banker for the climb to Talerddig.

1 September 1959

37 The driver is looking ahead and the fireman is about to swing a shovel-ful of coal into the firebox of No. 46116 **Irish Guardsman** as this London to Holyhead express has just crossed the River Dee outside Chester.

2 September 1959

38 The speed restriction sign showing a maximum speed of 50 mph for the points at Weaver Junction is just visible at the left of the picture. No. 45580 **Burma** has crossed the River Weaver with a down express.

5 September 1959

39 In the opposite direction and taken from the same spot No. 46243 **City of Lancaster** hurries by with the up *Royal Scot,* the engine being in maroon livery.

5 September 1959

40   Another special, this time for the Talyllyn Railway Preservation Society from London to Towyn for the Annual General Meeting. 'Dukedogs' Nos. 9004 and 9014 speed down the valley from Cemmaes Road to Machynlleth.

26 September 1959

41   Cup Final day at Wembley and as Wolverhampton Wanderers were in the match a number of specials were run. This one is taken near Claydon Crossing to the north of Banbury and the tender of No. 6006 **King George I** has been suitably decorated.

6 May 1960

My only visit to the Somerset and Dorset was to see a special hauled by S & D 2-8-0 No. 53807 leave the city of Bath. Here is the engine at Bath Green Park Shed after being prepared for the run. Note the tablet exchange apparatus on the tender.

14 May 1960

No. 40634 was originally built as a ... 40700 was the last of the class built for the LMSR. Both engines of course were made after grouping and it looks as if 40700 is out of use due to the chimney being covered over.

14 May 1960

44   In a corner of the Shed at Bath was this delightful Johnson design
(Midland Railway) 0-4-4 tank engine awaiting its fate.

14 May 1960

45   Now here is a sight worth waiting for as No. 53807 comes up the
gradient out of Bath in the glorious sunshine. Note the fire irons on the
top of the tender and the clean design of this engine.

14 May 1960

Following the special was the *Pines Express* and after that this local train stopping at all stations. The 0-6-0 No. 44557 looks a bit grimy but the coaches are just out of the works in Southern green. The location is of course to the south of Midford Station.

14 May 1960

arrive behind No. 6932 **Burwarton Hall.** It is approaching the city from the London direction and is probably a holiday extra from the south.

14 May 1960

48 The final call for the day was at Stratton St Margaret outside Swindon and the daily running in turn is coming in from the east behind 2-8-0 No. 2892.

14 May 1960

49 An historic view of the rebuilding of Coventry station. With a local train in the down platform the tank engine and coach were used to take parcels from one side to the other. The picture is looking south and I like the two men chasing a copy of the daily paper across the track!

we had our summer holiday in North Wales and although mainline gauge the Festiniog has been a favourite for many years and I cannot help including this one. The bridge in the background had just been rebuilt and necessitated a temporary level crossing shown to the right of the picture. **Taliesin** approaches Boston Lodge with a return afternoon train.

7 June 1960

way to Bangor. With a handsome looking 2-6-4 tank engine No. 42074 it makes a fine sight in the early morning.

10 June 1960

52 The place Leamington Spa GWR shed. The engine a Stanier 2-8-0 just received back from Crewe works after overhaul. Alas it must have run a hot big end as the connecting rod is lying on the ground protected by a couple of lamps.

19 June 1960

53 The next four pictures were taken on the visit to Crewe to see how the electrification was progressing. The *Pines Express* approaches behind a very dirty 'Britannia' class Pacific No. 70042 **Lord Roberts** from the Manchester end.

25 June 1960

At the south end of the station one of the new PARKER banking
service has arrived with a passenger train. The *Merseyside Express* runs
through behind No. D.255.

25 June 1960

would come back in the afternoon. A request to the fireman for smoke
during a chat at Chester did not provide much black on the troughs outside the city.

25 June 1960

56 The fireman leans out of the cab of No. 46241 **City of Edinburgh** as water is picked up by the scoop under the tender.

25 June 1960

57 20.00 hrs on a summer evening at Liverpool Street Station with one aim in view — to see the two immaculate station pilots, 0-6-0 No. 68619 in Great Eastern livery makes interesting contrast to No. 70040 **Clive of India** with a boat express.

58 And here they are together with the driver of No. 69614 oiling up the motion. I gathered from conversation with the crews that the reason the engines were kept so clean was that extra payment was given.

28 June 1960

59 And so to the final picture with quite a line up at 20.35 in the evening. Perhaps I can leave you to work out the classes of all the engines.

28 June 1960

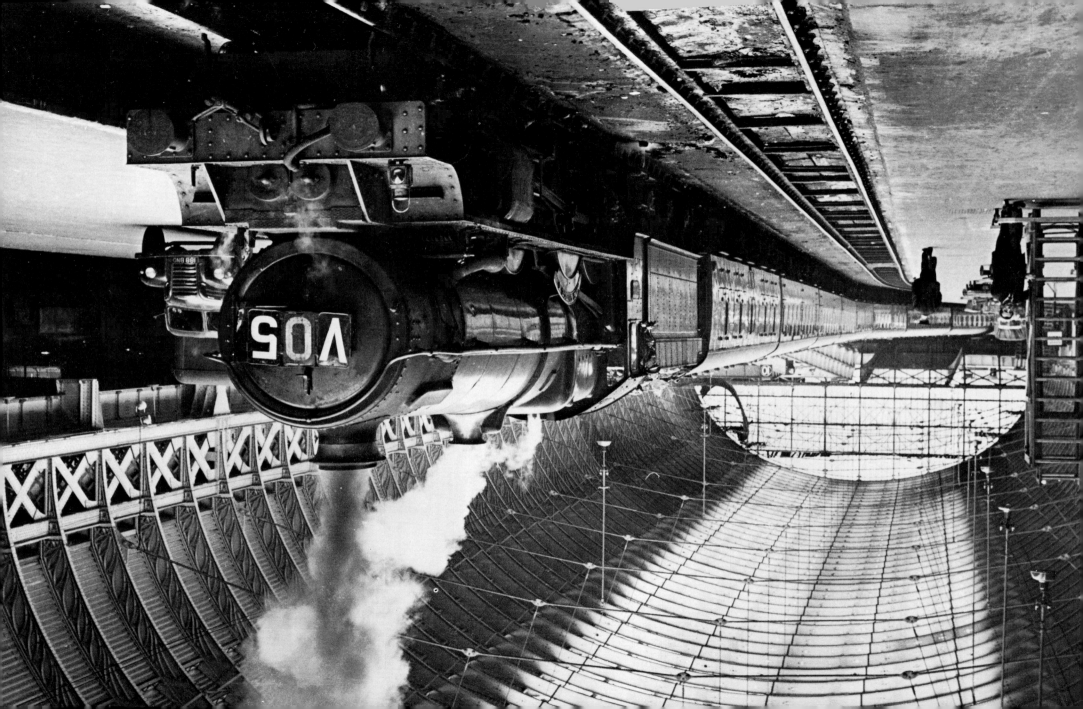

60 I came back to London a few days later behind No. 6006 **King George I** on the 11.35 Wolverhampton to Paddington and here is the train after arrival.

30 June 1960

61 Down at Old Oak Common an Austerity 2-8-0 has the fire lit up and clouds of acrid smoke are shown coming out of the chimney. Was it the dirt and long hours of work which killed the steam engine? No, I believe it had served the purpose for which it was designed for well over a hundred years and died a natural death from our advance in technology. You cannot go backwards or stay the same but only progress to better things.

30 June 1960

62 Scenes such as this make romantic viewing and memories linger on but I am sure no one would wish to return to the darkest corners of Old Oak Common Shed.

30 June 1960

63 No. 3440 **City of Truro** climbs out of Leamington, wrong line working, with a Stephenson Locomotive Society Special from Birmingham to Swindon. Quite a crowd on the footplate!

4 September 1960

64

A week later the Midland Compound was in action on a special from Nottingham to Swindon via Reading, Basingstoke, Andover and up the MSWJR. The Compound came off at Oxford, I believe, and ran light to Swindon to await the return trip. Here is the train on Aynho water troughs to the south of Banbury on a cloudless day with no exhaust.

11 September 1960

65

Now down-graded and single track from Princes Risborough to Aynho Junction, the shortest route by the Western Region to Birmingham was used to capacity eighteen years ago. In this shot No. 6017 **King Edward IV** with steam to spare approaches Beaconsfield with the 14.10 Paddington to Birkenhead.

17 September 1960

Another running in turn which was a regular feature at Crewe works was an early morning train stopping at all stations to Shrewsbury. In this view No. 46245 **City of London** is nearing the outskirts of Shrewsbury on a misty morning.

In chalk at the bottom of the smokebox of No. 4918 **Dartington Hall** is written 'NOT TO BE BLOWN', and I wonder what this can mean. The scene is of course Shrewsbury looking south with Class 5 No. 45395 awaiting departure for Crewe.

68 Another engine just out of Crewe works is this Class 5 No. 45448 seen at Shrewsbury shed in the evening awaiting its next call of duty.

24 September 1960

69 This route from Shrewsbury to Hereford and South Wales rarely sees trains as long as this one today. Hauled by No. 5044 **Earl of Dunraven,** it is near Stapleton and will soon be starting the climb up to Church Stretton.

70 Another favourite spot half way down Hatton Bank as the up trains have usually shut off steam and a nice trail of black smoke flows along the top of the coaches. No. 6017 **King Edward IV** has the 11.00 from Birmingham Snow Hill to Paddington.

Knowing that No. 46203 **Princess Margaret Rose** was in Crewe works for overhaul I arranged to be allowed to take some photographs of the engine after it emerged from the paint shop. Here it is ex-works for the last time in green livery and it is good to know that it survives today.

7 February 1961

72 Thinking back over the years it is not always easy to locate the exact spot where some of the pictures were taken. At the back of Edge Hill Shed in Liverpool 0-8-0 No. 49002 passes by with a freight train heading for the city.

73 I then went down to Liverpool Lime Street Station to see a well groomed 'Scot' leaving on a train to Chester. No. 46163 **Civil Service Rifleman** simmers away underneath the overall roof of the station.

18 February 1961

74 In the afternoon I went to Chester and the state of these two engines of similar class is interesting, watched by engine spotters of the day. 2-6-4 tank engine No. 42183 on the left and No. 42583 on the right.

18 February 1961

75 With less than a year of its life left before withdrawal No. 6006 **King George I** climbs out of Harbury Tunnel with the 11.00 Birmingham Snow Hill to Paddington. This engine was the first of the 'Kings' to be withdrawn in February 1962.

29 March 1961

76 Cup Final day again but this time all the specials came down the Great Central mainline. No. 46160 **Queen Victoria's Rifleman** has just come through Catesby Tunnel after the climb from Rugby. Go and have a look at the scene today.

6 April 1961

77 I am standing by the bridge which carries the Stratford-upon-Avon and Midland Junction Railway over the Great Central. 2-6-4 tank engine No. 67740 heads south and will most likely take the branch to Banbury.

6 April 1961

78 The approach to Leamington Spa from the south as seen by the railway traveller used to be pretty grim. This picture shows some of the demolition taking place at that time for a new Industrial Estate to be built. No. 2211 runs past the signals set for entry to the Great Western Shed. I wonder if the coach was preserved!

12 April 1961

The last year of working The Inter-City by *King Edward VIII* leaving Leamington Spa on a dull evening. The scene has altered dramatically today.

26 May 1961

My Southern content really started when we took to the Isle of Wight for holidays each year and like many others I fell for the Island railways. In 1961 Ryde Pier Head to Cowes and also Ventnor were still in full swing with the engines in a reasonable state of cleanliness. The 18.30 from Ryde to Cowes has just left Smallbrook Junction with the next stop Ashey Station.

20 June 1961

81

A broadside view of an O2 at speed approaching Ryde St John's Road Station with a train from Ventnor and hauled by No. 22 **Brading.**

21 June 1961

82 A few minutes later No. 25 **Godshill** appears with a coal train from Medina Wharf up the river near Cowes. This will be for the locomotive depot at Ryde.

21 June 1961

83 The coal train has now been split up and it is seen on the left of the picture. Passing by on the 18.25 from Ryde to Ventnor is No. 29 **Alverstone.**

21 June 1961

84 One of the routes to the Isle of Wight is Lymington to Yarmouth and here the cars are queueing for the ferry. A nice collection of vehicles but the push-pull from Brockenhurst should be the attraction, hauled by 0-4-4 tank engine No. 30133.

24 June 1961

vice trains were running. Here No. 30781 **Sir Aglovale** is approaching Brockenhurst Station with the 09.30 Bournemouth to Wolverhampton.

24 June 1961

It turned out to be a cloudless day and very hot with trains going past
every few minutes. No. 34037 **Clovelly** has just passed Brockenhurst
with the 10.15 Bournemouth to Waterloo.

24 June 1961

The 'Schools' class 4-4-0 express engines were still running and one or
two were on the trains for the Isle of Wight. No. 30927 **Clifton** is
slowing down for the Brockenhurst stop with the 9.55 Woking to
Weymouth.

24 June 1961

...ton with the 13.05 Bournemouth to Waterloo.

24 June 1961

30855 **Robert Blake** with the 12.20 Waterloo to Bournemouth.

24 June 1961

approaches the signals which have just been cleared. The train is the 14.05 from Eastleigh to Bournemouth and as you probably know the engine is in preservation on the Mid-Hants line.

24 June 1961

9? Later in the afternoon I took a train to Bradford Road Station and walked into the New Forest to see the trains. No. 35017 **Belgian Marine** heads for London with the up *Bournemouth Belle*.

24 June 1961

with the 10.00 Bradford Exchange to Poole.

24 June 1961

603 Squadron approaches the station at speed with a returning excursion.

24 June 1961

94 Whilst waiting for my train to Lymington No. 35021 **New Zealand Line**
stopped at the station with the 17.30 from Waterloo to Bournemouth.
No. 30133 arrives from Lymington.

24 June 1961

95 Back on the Isle of Wight No. 16 **Ventnor** approaches Shanklin
Junction with the 08.25 Ryde to Ventnor train. Note the fixed distant
signals on the road bridge.

28 June 1961

96 And for the last picture in this volume No. 21 **Sandown** is coming down the bank from Smallbrook Junction to Ryde St John's Road station with an evening train from Ventnor. Just for once I failed to record the date!